## Other Kaplan Books for Spanish Learners

Spanish Verb Flashcards Flip-O-Matic

Lazarillo de Tormes: A Kaplan Spanish-Language Vocabulary Building Novel

KAPLAN

Test Prep and Admissions

# Spanish Vocabulary Flashcards Flip-O-Matic

Compiled by Ken Stewart

Simon & Schuster

New York · London · Sydney · Toronto

Kaplan Publishing
Published by Simon & Schuster
1230 Avenue of the Americas
New York, NY 10020



Editor: Ruth Baygell
Production Manager: Michael Shevlin
Executive Editor: Jennifer Farthing
Interior Page Design: Dave Chipps

September 2004

10 9 8 7 6 5 4 3 2 1

Manufactured in the United States of America
Published simultaneously in Canada

ISBN 0-7432-6038-4

# HOW TO USE THIS BOOK

This book will provide you with a powerful word arsenal that will complement your Spanish language skills. It offers words that tend to appear frequently in everyday conversation, and on the challenging SAT II, AP, and CLEP Spanish exams. While it is impossible to predict exactly which words will appear on an exam, having a broad and varied vocabulary is bound to improve your performance. A superior vocabulary is the hallmark of the best essays and speech samples.

**If you are taking an AP Spanish Exam:** Though you will not be tested on vocabulary *per se*, a wide-ranging vocabulary is essential for attaining a high score. In fact, having an extensive vocabulary can sometimes compensate for weaknesses in other areas. Responses are scored not only on your control of syntax, but also on the level of fluency and richness of vocabulary with which you deliver your answer.

**If you are taking an SAT II, CLEP, or another college placement test:** The vocabulary that appears on these tests tends to be assessed in discrete sentences that offer little context. In order to score well, it is essential that you learn as many advanced words as possible. Likewise, in the reading comprehension sections, you must be able to guess intelligently about unfamiliar words. Test items can be literary or journalistic and may also include day-to-day language.

**If you are learning Spanish vocabulary on your own:** Since you do not have the classroom contact to reinforce the meanings of these words or to use them in context, it is imperative that you study these words cumulatively and consistently. To contextualize your new vocabulary, keep a journal that uses the new words in personalized sentences. With the word *travieso* (daring, mischievous), for instance, you could write, “Mi hermanito Travis es travieso.” Try making a mental link between the word’s meaning and something you will remember.

# FORMAT OF THE BOOK

This book provides a broad array of word types: nouns, verbs, adjectives, idioms, adverbs, prepositions, conjunctions, and adverbial conjunctions. Particular attention is given to advanced verbs and sophisticated adjectives since they tend to produce a more impressive sentence, whether spoken or written. The appropriate part of speech and a sample sentence have also been included, so that you can better contextualize and understand the meaning and usage of each word.

The vocabulary words here are organized according to their part of speech: noun, verb, adjective, adverb, conjunction, or idiom. You will notice, however, that they are scrambled at random within each category. This is to help you focus on the individual word, its meaning, and its context. The idea is that words listed alphabetically are harder to distinguish and learn, since they look and sound alike. Choose to study the words in any order and to start on any page. Remember to flip the book over and study the other half. Once you have mastered a word, clip or fold the corner back so that you can zip right through the book focusing only on unfamiliar words.

# DECODING THE MEANINGS OF WORDS

Recognizing common prefixes, suffixes, and roots of words can be a useful tool in deciphering a word's meaning as well as its part of speech. Take the verb *tener*. While you should know that it means "to have," it also is the equivalent in English of *-tain*, as in "entertain." If you begin by identifying a word's root and then determining if a prefix or suffix has been added, you will quickly start to assimilate new words into your active vocabulary. Consider how many new words can be formed just by adding a different prefix to the verb *tener*:

| | |
|---|---|
| **entre**tener: | to entertain |
| **man**tener: | to maintain |
| **de**tener: | to detain |
| **re**tener: | to retain |
| **ob**tener: | to obtain |
| **con**tener: | to contain |
| **sos**tener: | to sustain |
| **abs**tener: | to abstain |

**Words that end in these suffixes are nouns:**

| | |
|---|---|
| -ción = -tion: | la construcción |
| -ador = -ator: | el dictador |
| -encia = -ence, -ency | la apariencia, la residencia |
| -fía = -phy: | la bibliografía |
| -ismo = -ism: | el capitalismo |
| -io = -ium: | el medio |
| -dad, -tad = -ty | la universidad, la libertad |

**Words that end in these suffixes are adjectives:**

| | |
|---|---|
| -oso = -ous: | generoso |
| -ivo = -ive: | pasivo |
| -cial = -tial: | parcial |
| -az = -acious: | locuaz |
| -orio = -ory: | obligatorio |
| -ente = -ent: | evidente |

**Words that end in –*mente* are adverbs:**

| | |
|---|---|
| -mente = -ly: | apasionadamente, francamente |

Additionally, many adverbs in Spanish are formed by adding prepositions (*de*, *con*, *a*) to nouns or adjectives:

de prisa = in a hurry

con cuidado = carefully

a tiempo = on time

# GENDER OF NOUNS

There are a few basic rules about the gender of nouns in Spanish. As you probably know, nouns ending in *-o* are generally masculine, while nouns ending in *-a* are almost always feminine. By learning the suffixes below, you will strengthen your ability to guess intelligently about a new word's gender. Using the correct gender is important, as basic errors in articles and agreement tend to detract from the overall quality of an essay or conversation.

Nouns that end in these suffixes are almost always **masculine**:

| | |
|---|---|
| -ón: | el tiburón, el salchichón |
| -aje: | el peaje, el pasaje |
| -or: | el gobernador, el temor |
| -al: | el tamal, el hospital |
| -ema, -oma: | el sistema, el idioma |

Nouns that end in these suffixes are almost always **feminine**:

| | |
|---|---|
| -dad, -tad: | la honestidad, la lealtad |
| -ción, -sión: | la satisfacción, la lesión |
| -ie | la carie, la superficie |
| -tud | la magnitud, la juventud |
| -itis | la artritis, la bronquitis |
| -umbre | la incertidumbre, la muchedumbre |

Nouns that end in these suffixes can be either **masculine or feminine**:

| | |
|---|---|
| -ante: | el/la estudiante |
| -ista: | el/la dentista |
| -ente: | el/la adolescente |

Some nouns are **invariable** and are therefore applied to both genders regardless of whether they refer to a male or female. These must be memorized since there is no way to determine their gender. The article always remains the same for these nouns.

la víctima

la serpiente

el ángel

el personaje

la araña

# MEMORIZATION TECHNIQUES

- Approach the words systematically. Look for common roots, prefixes, suffixes, and particularly, cognates of English words to help you make intelligent choices.
- Look for contextualized clues. Vocabulary words do not occur in isolation and can often have more than one meaning. Therefore, look beyond the literal translation of any given word.
- Review the words in short study sessions. 15 minutes of intense study each night is better than hours of study just prior to taking a test.
- Consider color coding your Flip-O-Matic book. To reinforce the gender of nouns or the parts of speech, use highlighters to color code the words categorically.
- Label your surroundings. Making labels or stickers for household items, classroom objects, etc., can reinforce your long-term memory of many common nouns.
- Using the words, create sentences that will be meaningful to you. After reading the sentence that demonstrates the meaning of each word in the book, write your own sentence so as to personalize the word.
- Say the words aloud as you flip through the book. Repetition will reinforce the words and help with retention and pronunciation.

- Read voraciously. Brain research shows that reading comprehension and vocabulary acquisition are closely related. Seeing words in context will help your diction and you are more likely to use the word correctly in the future.

- Take 5. Take 5 idioms or conjunctions from the book that may be applicable to many contexts and learn them thoroughly. Plan to put them in your next writing or speaking assignment.

- Combine your grammar reviews with new vocabulary. As you continue to learn new grammar, you should seek to include new vocabulary. For example, if you are learning comparisons, create more unique answers than *más inteligente que.* Consider: Pablo es *más sagaz, más erudito, más culto que* Roberto.

- Practice with a friend. Together you can create new contexts for the words that you're more likely to remember. It will make learning more fun as well.

## la frontera

(noun)

---

**so that, in order that**

Ponte una chaqueta *para que* no tengas frío.

Put on a jacket so that you're not cold.

**border**

El Río Bravo forma *la frontera* entre los Estados Unidos y México.

The Rio Grande forms the border between the United States and Mexico.

---

**para que**

(adverbial conj.)

**el desarrollo**

(noun)

**as soon as**

Te avisaré *luego que* reciba las noticias.

I will let you know as soon as I receive the news.

**development**

El buen *desarrollo* del los niños depende de la atención de los padres.

Proper development of children depends on the attention of their parents.

---

**luego que**

(adverbial conj.)

**la amenaza**

(noun)

**provided that**

Celebraremos la boda afuera *con tal que* no llueva.

We will celebrate the wedding outside provided that it doesn't rain.

**threat**

La falta de agua potable en muchos países presenta una *amenaza* a la salud pública.

Lack of drinkable water in many countries presents a threat to public health.

---

**con tal que**

(adverbial conj.)

## la sequía

(noun)

---

**unless**

No hace falta esperar en esa cola tan larga para pasar por la aduana *a no ser que* uno tenga algo que declarar.

It's not necessary to wait in that long line for customs unless one has items to declare.

**drought**

Los granjeros temen que la cosecha sea menos abundante debido a la *sequía*.

Farmers fear that the harvest will be less abundant due to the drought.

**a no ser que**

(conj.)

# la píldora

(noun)

**but [rather]**

El clima de Valencia no es húmedo *sino* seco.

Valencia's climate is not humid, but [rather] dry.

**pill**

El médico le recetó una *píldora* nueva para la alta presión sanguínea.

The doctor prescribed a new pill for high blood pressure.

---

**sino**

(conj.)

**la despedida**

(noun)

---

**given that**

*Dado que* ya es verano, se abrirá la piscina pronto.

Given that it's already summer, the swimming pool will open soon.

**farewell**

La *despedida* fue más triste porque Paula temía más nunca ver a su novio.

The farewell was sadder because Paula was afraid that she'd never see her boyfriend again.

**dado que**

(conj.)

**el sótano**

(noun)

**since; inasmuch**

*Desde que* nació el bebé, nadie en la casa duerme toda la noche.

Since the baby was born, nobody in the house sleeps through the night.

**basement**

El *sótano* amplio sirve para guardar todos los adornos que ya no usamos.

The large basement serves to keep all the decorations we are no longer using.

**desde que**

(conj.)

**el semáforo**

(noun)

**through; throughout**

*A través de* la historia hasta las grandes civilizaciones se han caído.

Throughout history even the greatest of civilizations have fallen.

**traffic light**

El bulevar tiene tantos *semáforos* que tarda mucho en llegar al centro comercial.

The boulevard has so many traffic lights that it takes a long time to get to the shopping mall.

**a través de**

(prep.)

**la taquilla**

(noun)

**at the beginning of**

*A principios de* octubre vamos a hacer una excursión al Gran Cañón.

At the beginning of October we're going to take a trip to the Grand Canyon.

**box office; ticket window**

Después de hacer cola por horas, cuando llegamos a la *taquilla* ya no quedaban entradas.

After waiting in line for hours, when we arrived at the ticket window there were no tickets left.

---

**a principios de**

(prep.)

# el ayuntamiento

(noun)

**on top of**

*Encima del* campanario la cigüeña hizo un nido.

On top of the belfry the stork built a nest.

**town hall**

El *ayuntamiento* queda enfrente de la catedral en la plaza.

Town hall sits in front of the catedral on the public square.

**encima de**

(prep.)

**la cebolla**

(noun)

**according to**

*Según* las encuestas, la economía se está mejorando.

According to the surveys, the economy is improving.

**onion**

Me puse a llorar cuando picaba la *cebolla* para la ensalada.

I began to cry when I diced the onion for the salad.

---

**según**

(prep.)

**from ... on, beginning**

*A partir del* año entrante, el restaurante no va a aceptar tarjetas de crédito.

Beginning next year, the restaurant will no longer accept credit cards.

**la cesta**

(noun)

**basket**

Ana María me regaló una *cesta* de frutas cuando yo estaba hospitalizado.

Ana Maria gave me a basket of fruit as a gift when I was hospitalized.

---

**a partir de**

(prep.)

**el éxito**

(noun)

**next to**

Coloqué la alfombra nueva *junto a* la chimenea.

I placed the new rug next to the fireplace.

**success**

Celia Cruz, cantante cubana, gozó de mucho *éxito* durante más de tres décadas.

Celia Cruz, the Cuban singer, enjoyed much success for more than three decades.

**junto a**

(prep.)

## el socorro

(noun)

**outside of**

*Fuera de* la geología, Teodoro no sabe mucho de las ciencias.

Outside of geology, Teodoro doesn't know much about science.

**rescue, help, aid**

La niña gritó "*socorro*" para llamar la atención del salvavidas.

The girl shouted "help" to get the lifeguard's attention.

---

**fuera de**

(prep.)

**about, concerning**

El decano dio un discurso *acerca de* los programas que se ofrecen en la universidad.

The dean gave a talk about the programs that are offered at the university.

---

**el acero**

(noun)

**steel**

La producción de *acero* bajó bastante con la invención de nuevos materiales más económicos.

Steel production fell substantially with the invention of new and more economic materials.

**acerca de**

(prep.)

**el algodón**

(noun)

**toward**

Los girasoles se giran *hacia* el sol.

Sunflowers turn toward the sun.

**cotton**

Me gusta más el chaleco de *algodón* puesto que tengo alergia a la lana.

I prefer the cotton vest since I am allergic to wool.

**hacia**

(prep.)

**la ventaja**

(noun)

**around**

Magallanes fue el primero para navegar *alrededor del* mundo.

Magellan was the first to sail around the world.

**advantage**

Hablar más de un idioma es de gran *ventaja* hoy en día.

Speaking more than one language is a great advantage today.

**alrededor de**

(prep.)

**el comportamiento**

(noun)

**with regard to**

*En cuanto a* la economía, todo depende de la tasa de interés.

With regard to the economy, everything depends on the interest rate.

**behavior**

Los zoólogos han comprobado que el *comportamiento* de los monos se parece al nuestro.

Zoologists have proven that the behavior of monkeys is similar to ours.

---

**en cuanto a**

(prep.)

## el recorrido

(noun)

**almost, nearly**

Las Panteras *por poco* ganan el partido en los últimos segundos.

The Panthers nearly won the game in the final seconds.

**route, trip**

Hicimos un *recorrido* turístico por Francia e Italia el verano pasado.

We took a pleasure trip to France and Italy last summer.

**por poco**

(adv.)

**el cuero**

(noun)

---

**unfortunately**

*Desgraciadamente* no teníamos tiempo para recorrer todo el museo.

Unfortunately we didn't have time to go through the entire museum.

**leather, hide**

Parece hipócrita ser vegetariano y llevar puesto un abrigo de *cuero*.

It seems hypocritical to be a vegetarian and to wear a leather coat.

---

**desgraciadamente**

(*adv.*)

**la talla**

(noun)

**perhaps; by chance**

¿*Acaso* tienes cambio por un billete de 100 euros?

By chance do you have change for 100 euros?

**[clothing] size**

Para mi cumpleaños me regalaron una camiseta muy bonita, pero lamentablemente no es mi *talla*.

For my birthday they gave me a very pretty shirt, but unfortunately it isn't my size.

**acaso**

(*adv.*)

**el atardecer**

(noun)

**maybe; perhaps**

*Quizás* haya vida en otros planetas.

Perhaps there is life on other planets.

**dusk, twilight**

Al *atardecer*, el barco se desapareció más allá del horizonte.

At dusk, the boat disappeared beyond the horizon.

**quizás**

(*adv.*)

**la censura**

(noun)

**perhaps, at best**

Voy a estudiar en el extranjero cuando vaya a la universidad, *a lo mejor* en Costa Rica.

I am going to study abroad when I go to college, perhaps in Costa Rica.

**censorship**

La *censura* va en contra de los principios democráticos.

Censorship goes against democratic principles.

---

**a lo mejor**

(*adv.*)

## la herramienta

(noun)

---

**such that; so that**

Estela me dio el dinero *de modo que* yo pude comprar las entradas al concierto de jazz.

Estela gave me the money so that I could buy the tickets to the jazz concert.

**tool**

En la caja llena de llaves y alicates, Anita no tenía la *herramienta* necesaria para arreglar la tele.

In the box full of wrenches and pliers, Anita didn't have the tool necessary to fix the television.

---

**de modo que**

(*adv.*)

**la huella**

(noun)

---

**early**

Es mejor que llegues *temprano* al estadio para conseguir un asiento en la primera fila.

It's better that you arrive early at the stadium to get a front-row seat.

**track; footprint**

Sabíamos que había osos en el bosque por las *huellas* que dejaron en el lodo.

We knew that there were bears in the forest by the footprints that they left in the mud.

**temprano**

(*adv.*)

**la jaula**

(noun)

---

**happily**

Los pájaros estaban cantando *alegremente* cuando me desperté esta mañana.

The birds were singing happily when I woke up this morning.

**cage**

El canario estará seguro en esta *jaula*.

The canary will be safe in this cage.

---

**alegremente**

(*adv.*)

**el aporte**

(noun)

**hardly, barely**

*Apenas* nos habíamos sentado a cenar cuando el teléfono sonó.

We had barely sat down to dinner when the phone rang.

**contribution**

Uno de los *aportes* de los indígenas al Viejo Mundo fue el tomate.

One of the contributions of the indigenous people to the Old World was the tomato.

**apenas**

(adv.)

**bitterly**

El noviazgo terminó *amargamente* después que Alejandro dejó plantada a Sonia.

The engagement ended bitterly after Alejandro stood up Sonia.

---

**los impuestos**

(noun)

**taxes**

Para pasar por el Canal de Panamá, los buques tienes que pagar *impuestos* altos.

To pass through the Panama Canal, ships have to pay high taxes.

**amargamente**

(adv.)

**la cicatriz**

(noun)

**since**

Lo he conocido *desde* que éramos niños.

I have known him since we were children.

**scar**

Aunque se curó la lesión, la *cicatriz* permanece en la mano.

Although the wound was healed, the scar remained on his hand.

---

**desde**

(*adv.*)

**el porvenir**

(noun)

---

**still, yet**

*Todavía* no he visto la última película de Pedro Almodóvar.

I still haven't seen Pedro Almodóvar's latest movie.

**future**

En el *porvenir* se podrá contar con transporte más rápido entre los distintos países del mundo.

In the future one will be able to rely on faster transportation between the different countries of the world.

**todavía**

(*adv.*)

## el castigo

(noun)

**slowly**

El professor habló *lentamente* para que todos pudieran tomar apuntes durante la conferencia.

The professor spoke slowly so that everyone could take notes during the lecture.

**punishment**

El *castigo* que se decidió fue tres años en la cárcel.

The punishment that was decided was three years in jail.

---

**lentamente**

(*adv.*)

**el delantal**

(noun)

**too [much]**

Los gastos son *demasiado* altos para el ingreso que ganamos.

The expenses are too high for the income that we earn.

**apron**

Es mejor que te pongas un *delantal* mientras estás preparando la cena para que no te manches la camisa.

It is best that you put on an apron while you are preparing dinner so that you don't stain your shirt.

**demasiado**

(*adv.*)

## el rincón

(noun)

**in detail**

Velázquez retrató a la infanta Margarita *detalladamente*.

Velázquez portrayed the princess Margarita in detail.

**corner [of a room]**

Prefiero aquella mesa en el *rincón* donde hay menos ruido.

I prefer that table in the corner where there is less noise.

**detalladamente**

(*adv.*)

**efficiently, efficaciously**

Si todos manejáramos autos que anduvieran más *eficazmente*, se reduciría el consumo de petróleo.

If all of us drove cars that ran more efficiently, oil consumption would be reduced.

## los alrededores

(noun)

**suburbs; surrounding areas; outskirts**

Los *alrededores* de la ciudad han crecido hacia el sur en los últimos años.

The suburbs of the city have grown (out) to the south in the last few years.

---

**eficazmente**

(*adv.*)

**el terremoto**

(noun)

---

**swiftly**

Los jinetes cabalgaron *velozmente* a través de la llanura.

The horseman galloped swiftly across the plain.

**earthquake**

Suele haber muchos *terremotos* a través de los Andes.

There tend to be many earthquakes throughout the Andes.

---

**velozmente**

(*adv.*)

**la pesadilla**

(noun)

---

**currently**

*Actualmente* el euro vale más de un dólar estadounidense.

Currently, the euro is worth more than a U.S. dollar.

**nightmare**

La niña sufrió de una *pesadilla* tras otra al ver la película de horror.

The girl suffered one nightmare after another upon seeing the horror movie.

---

**actualmente**

(*adv.*)

## un sindicato

(noun)

---

**besides, in addition to**

*Además* de los exámenes finales, me toca entregar un informe escrito sobre Lorca.

In addition to the final exams, I have to turn in a paper on Lorca.

**labor union**

Los obreros pertenecen a un *sindicato* para proteger sus derechos.

The workers belong to a labor union to protect their rights.

**además**

(*adv.*)

## el aceite

(noun)

**no matter how**

*Por* más *que* trates, no creo que la ropa quepa en la valija.

No matter how much you try, I don't think the clothing will fit in the suitcase.

**oil**

Eche un poco de *aceite* en la sartén para que la tortilla de patatas no se pegue.

Put a little oil in the skillet so that the potato omelet will not stick.

---

**por . . . que**

(idiom)

## la factura

(noun)

**to be in style**

Como Cecilia trabaja en el almacén de ropa para damas, sus faldas siempre *están de moda.*

Since Cecilia works in a women's clothing store, her skirts are always in style.

**invoice; bill; statement**

Es aconsejable pedirle una *factura* a la dependienta por si acaso hay que devolver alguna prenda.

It is advisable to ask for an invoice from the clerk in case it is necessary to return an article of clothing.

**estar de moda**

(idiom)

## el reto

(noun)

**in fact**

Sabemos que muchos dinosaurios eran vegetarianos; *en efecto*, muy pocos eran carnívoros.

We know that many dinosaurs were vegetarians; in fact, very few were carnivores.

**challenge**

Subir a la cumbre del volcán es un *reto* que pocas personas aceptarán.

Climbing to the summit of the volcano is a challenge that few people will accept.

---

**en efecto**

(idiom)

**to be someone's turn**

*A ti te toca* lavar los platos puesto que yo los lavé anoche.

It is your turn to wash the plates since I washed them last night.

# el golpe

(noun)

**hit, punch, or blow**

El *golpe* en la frente me dio una jaqueca tremenda.

A blow to the forehead gave me a tremendous migraine.

**tocarle a uno**

(idiom)

**la queja**

(noun)

---

**to drop**

Soy tan torpe; *dejé caer* el jarrón que hice en la clase de cerámica.

I am so clumsy; I dropped the vase that I made in ceramics class.

**complaint**

Quiero hablar con el gerente, por favor. Tenemos una *queja*.

I want to speak with the manager, please. We have a complaint.

---

**dejar caer**

(idiom)

## el aumento

(noun)

**to deal with; to have to do with**

La portada del libro no *tiene* nada *que ver con* el argumento.

The cover of the book has nothing to do with the plot.

**increase**

Debido al *aumento* de interés en la película, se decidió pasarla dos días más.

Due to the increase in the film’s popularity, it was decided to show it two more days.

---

**tener que ver con**

(idiom)

**to blame**

Me fastidia que mi hermano me *eche la culpa* cada vez que llegamos tarde al colegio.

It annoys me that my brother blames me every time we arrive late to school.

# el escaparate

(noun)

**showcase, display window**

Aunque no teníamos dinero para comprar, disfrutamos de mirar las nuevas modas en los *escaparates*.

Although we didn't have money to buy, we enjoyed looking at the new fashions in the display windows.

---

**echar la culpa**

(idiom)

**el anciano**

(noun)

---

**to hear about**

*Oí hablar de* Simón Bolívar en mi curso de historia latinoamericana.

I heard about Simón Bolívar in my Latin American history course.

**elderly person**

Me agrada ayudar a los *ancianos* que viven en el asilo de la vejez cerca de mi casa.

It pleases me to help elderly people who live in the retirement home near my house.

---

**oír hablar de**

(idiom)

**more and more**

Se nota la presencia de los hispanos *cada vez más* en los Estados Unidos.

The presence of Hispanics is being noticed more and more in the United States.

**la acera**

(noun)

**sidewalk**

Es prohibido andar en monopatín en la *acera* porque es peligroso para los peatones.

It is prohibited to ride a skateboard on the sidewalk because it is dangerous for pedestrians.

---

**cada vez más**

(idiom)

**la vela**

(noun)

**to bump into; to come across**

Mientras leía los titulares del periódico, *di con* los resultados de la Copa Mundial.

While I was reading the newspaper headlines, I came across the results of the World Cup.

**candle**

Cuando se nos fue la luz, encendimos algunas *velas*.

When the power went out, we lit some candles.

---

**dar con**

(idiom)

# la carencia

(noun)

**one must; to have to**

*Hay que* tener cuidado caminando por esta senda porque está muy oscura.

One must be careful walking down this dark path.

**shortage, lack**

Debido a la *carencia* de agua, es mejor que tomes una ducha más rápida.

Due to a water shortage, it is better that you take a very quick shower.

---

**hay que**

(idiom)

**to face; to look out upon**

Quiero una habitación que *dé al* mar, por favor.

I want a room that looks out upon the ocean, please.

**la tela**

(noun)

**cloth, fabric**

El vestido de novia estaba hecho de una *tela* muy fina.

The wedding dress was made of a very fine fabric.

**dar a**

(idiom)

**from time to time**

Si no cambias el aceite en el auto *de vez en cuando*, le puede hacer daño al motor.

If you don't change the car oil from time to time it can do a lot of damage to the motor.

**el buzón**

(noun)

**mailbox**

El cartero dejó unas cartas importantes en el *buzón*.

The letter carrier left some important letters in the mailbox.

**de vez en cuando**

(idiom)

**to bear in mind; to take into account**

Hay que *tener en cuenta* el precio alto de quedarse en un hotel de lujo si tienes un presupuesto limitado.

One must bear in mind the high price of staying in a luxury hotel if you're on a limited budget.

---

**la señal**

(noun)

**signal, sign**

Espera hasta que oigas la *señal* antes de abrir la puerta del microondas.

Wait to hear the signal before opening the door of the microwave.

---

**tener en cuenta**

(idiom)

**el castillo**

(noun)

**willingly**

Siempre cumplo con mis quehaceres *de buena gana.*

I always do my chores willingly.

**castle**

Dicen que el *castillo* de Segovia es uno de los más pintorescos de España.

It is said that the castle in Segovia is one of the most picturesque in Spain.

**de buena gana**

(idiom)

**el sacerdote**

(noun)

**to have a good time**

Lo pasamos *bien* el en parque zoológico riéndonos de los monos.

We had a good time at the zoo laughing at the monkeys.

**priest**

El *sacerdote* oyó las confesiones de los penitentes.

The priest heard the confessions of the penitents.

---

**pasarlo bien**

(idiom)

**in cash**

Hay que pagar *en efectivo* en el mercado puesto que no se aceptan tarjetas de crédito.

You have to pay in cash at the market since they don't accept credit cards.

**la pantalla**

(noun)

**screen**

Me gusta ver películas en *pantalla* grande porque la acción es más realista.

I like seeing movies on a big screen because the action is more realistic.

---

**en efectivo**

(idiom)

**la carretera**

(noun)

**to tickle**

Mi hermano mayor siempre me *hacía cosquillas* y yo me reía a carcajadas.

My older brother always tickled me and I would laugh hysterically.

**highway**

Aunque ese camino es más pintoresco, se puede llegar más rápidamente yendo por la *carretera*.

Although this road is more picturesque, it is possible to arrive more quickly taking the highway.

**hacer cosquillas**

(idiom)

## la soledad

(noun)

**to rain cats and dogs**

Nos quedamos en el estadio mirando el partido a pesar de que *llovió a cántaros.*

We stayed in the stadium watching the ballgame in spite of it raining cats and dogs.

**loneliness, solitude**

La viuda sintió una profunda *soledad* al morirse su esposo.

The widow felt a profound loneliness upon the death of her husband.

**llover a cántaros**

(idiom)

**to be in mourning**

La viuda se vistió de negro porque *estaba de luto* durante el funeral.

The widow was dressed in black because she was in mourning during the funeral.

**el sorteo**

(noun)

**drawing; random selection**

Mis vecinos se ganaron dos pasajes a Orlando en un *sorteo*.

My neighbors won two tickets to Orlando in a drawing.

---

**estar de luto**

(idiom)

**el ejército**

(noun)

**to stick your foot in your mouth; to make an error**

A veces los políticos *meten la pata* cuando dan sus discursos en frente del público.

Sometimes politicians put their foot in their mouths when they give speeches in public.

**army**

Cuando el *ejército* se vio rodeado de tropas invasoras, se rindió.

When the army saw that it was surrounded by invading troops, it surrendered.

---

**meter la pata**

(idiom)

**el fondo**

(noun)

**to feel like [doing something]**

Al oír la salsa movida, *tuve ganas* de bailar.

Upon hearing the lively salsa, I felt like dancing.

**bottom, depth; background**

El barco destruido se hundió al *fondo* del mar.

The destroyed ship sank to the bottom of the sea.

---

**tener ganas de**

(idiom)

# el comedor

(noun)

**to wait in line**

Tuvimos que *hacer cola* por una hora en el aeropuerto antes de despachar el equipaje.

We had to wait in line for an hour at the airport before checking our baggage.

**dining room**

Toda la familia se juntó en el *comedor* para celebrar el cumpleaños de Cecilia.

The whole family got together in the dining room to celebrate Cecilia's birthday.

---

**hacer cola**

(idiom)

**la orilla**

(noun)

**face down**

Pon los naipes *boca abajo* en la mesa, por favor.

Put the cards face down on the table, please.

**shore, bank [of a river]**

Los pescadores ataron su bote a un árbol en la *orilla*.

The fishermen tied their boat to a tree on the bank.

**boca abajo**

(idiom)

**el auxilio**

(noun)

---

**to play the role**

Arturo *hizo el papel* de Don Juan en *El Burlador de Sevilla*.

Arturo played the role of Don Juan in *El Burlador de Sevilla*.

**aid, rescue, help**

Los paramédicos le dieron *auxilio* al señor que estaba desmayado.

The paramedics gave aid to the man who was unconscious.

---

**hacer el papel**

(idiom)

**el hogar**

(noun)

**to take a walk**

De niño, siempre me gustaba *dar un paseo* por el parque central.

As a child, I always enjoyed taking a walk in the central park.

**home**

Los Muñoz viven en un *hogar* muy acogedor en el valle Orosi.

The Muñoz family lives in a very cozy home in the Orosi Valley.

**dar un paseo**

(idiom)

**el tamaño**

(noun)

**in general**

*Por lo general*, me levanto a la misma hora cada día.

In general, I get up at the same time every day.

**size**

Quisiera una pizza de *tamaño* mediano con tomates y queso.

I would like a medium-size pizza with tomatoes and cheese.

**por lo general**

(idiom)

# la pereza

(noun)

**to take place**

La representación de la obra *tuvo lugar* en el anfiteatro porque hacía buen tiempo

The play was held in the amphitheater because the weather was good.

**laziness**

Por su *pereza* Jacinta no completó la solicitud para la beca.

Because of her laziness, Jacinta didn't complete the application for the scholarship.

---

**tener lugar**

(idiom)

**nonetheless; however**

Los Tigres gozaron de una temporada muy exitosa; *no obstante*, no ganaron el campeonato.

The Tigers enjoyed a very successful season; however, they didn't win the championship.

**el nido**

(noun)

**nest**

Las golondrinas hicieron un *nido* en lo alto del campanario.

The swallows made a nest on top of the bell tower.

---

**no obstante**

(idiom)

**el cansancio**

(noun)

**to become**

Mi abuela *se puso* deprimida al enterarse de las noticias.

My grandmother became depressed upon hearing the news.

**fatigue, tiredness**

Después de un vuelo de doce horas, el *cansancio* era insoportable; por eso, nos acostamos temprano.

After a 12-hour flight, the fatigue was unbearable; therefore, we went to bed early.

**ponerse (+ adj.)**

(idiom)

**to realize**

Apenas había entrado en el banco cuando *me di cuenta de* que se me había olvidado traer mi cheque.

I had barely entered the bank when I realized that I had forgotten to bring my check.

## el sello

(noun)

**stamp, seal**

Hace falta ponerle más *sellos* en este sobre porque es bastante grueso.

It is necessary to put more stamps on that envelope because it is fairly thick.

---

**darse cuenta de**

(idiom)

## la empresa

(noun)

**in spite of**

*A pesar de* su testimonio, el jurado decidió que él era culpable.

In spite of his testimony, the jury decided that he was guilty.

**corporation; big business**

Su marido trabajaba para una *empresa* internacional cuando vivieron en Londres.

Her husband was working for an international corporation when they lived in London.

**a pesar de**

(idiom)

## el tesoro

(noun)

**to carry out, accomplish**

Los soldados *llevaron a cabo* los mandatos del sargento.

The soldiers carried out the sergeant's orders.

**treasure**

Los piratas enterraron el *tesoro* en una isla donde nadie lo hallaría.

The pirates buried the treasure on an island where nobody would find it.

**llevar a cabo**

(idiom)

**el amanecer**

(noun)

**to be a fan of**

Mauricio sigue *siendo aficionado a* su equipo a pesar de que perdió el campeonato.

Mauricio continues to be a fan in spite of his team losing the championship.

**dawn**

El canto de los gallos nos despertó al *amanecer*.

The rooster's crow woke us up at dawn.

---

**ser aficionado a**

(idiom)

## el acontecimiento

(noun)

**at the same time; simultaneously**

La torta se ve riquísima, pero *a la misma vez*, no debo comerla porque engorda mucho.

The cake looks very tasty, but at the same time, I shouldn't eat it because it's very fattening.

**event, occurrence**

No pudimos encontrar donde estacionar el auto porque había algún *acontecimiento* en la plaza.

We weren't able to find a place to park the car because there was some event in the plaza.

---

**a la misma vez**

(idiom)

**to give birth**

Eugenia *dio a luz* a un bebé precioso después de estar de parto por cinco horas.

Eugenia gave birth to a beautiful baby after a five-hour labor.

**el apoyo**

(noun)

**support**

Sin el *apoyo* de sus partidarios, el candidato tuvo que abandonar su campaña.

Without the support of his followers, the candidate had to abandon his campaign.

**dar a luz**

(idiom)

**la etapa**

(noun)

---

**to have just (done something)**

*Acabábamos de* entrar en la sala cuando supimos que alguien nos había robado el televisor.

We had just entered the living room when we discovered that someone had stolen the TV.

**stage, phase**

La oruga pasa por varias *etapas* de metamorfosis antes de que sea una mariposa.

The caterpillar passes through various stages of metamorphosis before it becomes a butterfly.

---

**acabar de**

(idiom)

**la limosna**

(noun)

---

**to tease someone**

Patricia, no me estás hablando en serio. ¿Me estás *tomando el pelo?*

Patricia, you aren't serious. Are you teasing me?

**alms, charity**

La señora dio una *limosna* al pobre pordiosero.

The lady gave alms to the poor beggar.

---

**tomar el pelo**

(idiom)

**at once; right away**

Le dije a la víctima que no se preocupara ya que la ambulancia venía *en seguida*.

I told the victim not to worry since the ambulance was coming at once.

# el hilo

(noun)

**thread**

La costurera compró un *hilo* blanco para coser el agujero en la falda.

The dressmaker bought white thread to sew the hole in the skirt.

**en seguida**

(idiom)

## el tapiz

(noun)

**to be up to date; to be informed**

Los que leen el periódico diariamente *estarán al tanto* de los asuntos mundiales.

Those who read the newspaper daily will be up to date about world matters.

**tapestry**

Los *tapices* en el Palacio Real son obras de arte.

The tapestries in the Royal Palace are works of art.

**estar al tanto**

(idiom)

**to be worthwhile**

*Vale la pena* solicitar a varias universidades ya que la competencia para ser aceptado es cada vez más intensa.

It is worthwhile to apply to several universities since competition (to be accepted) is becoming more intense.

**la belleza**

(noun)

**beauty**

Ya que Sedona, Arizona es conocida por su *belleza* natural, vale la pena visitarla.

Since Sedona, Arizona is known for its natural beauty, it is a worthwhile visit.

---

**valer la pena**

(idiom)

## la catarata

(noun)

**to talk excessively**

Mi tía es una lora; *habla por los codos* con cualquiera.

My aunt is a chatterbox; she talks excessively with anyone.

**waterfall**

Las *cataratas* del Iguazú son mucho más altas que las de Niagara.

The waterfalls of Iguazú are much higher than those of Niagara.

---

**hablar por los codos**

(idiom)

**el nivel**

(noun)

---

**especially, above all**

Me fascinan las obras de El Greco, *sobre todo* "Vista de Toledo."

El Greco's works fascinate me, especially "View of Toledo."

**level**

Según su *nivel* de experiencia, se puede recibir un aumento de sueldo.

According to your level of experience, you can receive a raise in salary.

---

**sobre todo**

(idiom)

# el fracaso

(noun)

**beforehand**

El comité desarrolló un presupuesto *de antemano* para reducir los gastos.

The committee developed a budget beforehand to reduce expenses.

**failure**

La última canción de ese conjunto fue un *fracaso* total; casi nadie compró el disco compacto.

The last song of that group was a total failure; almost nobody bought the CD.

**de antemano**

(idiom)

**la flecha**

(noun)

**however, nevertheless**

Quisiera jugar al tennis, *sin embargo* no hay una cancha disponible.

I would like to play tennis, however, there is no court available.

**arrow**

La *flecha* amarilla indica la salida.

The yellow arrow indicates the exit.

---

**sin embargo**

(idiom)

## la esquina

(noun)

**to shake hands**

José es un tipo tan amable; siempre *da la mano* cuando saluda a sus compañeros.

José is so friendly; he always shakes hands when he meets his friends.

**street corner**

El autobús se paró en la *esquina* donde se subió un montón de personas.

The bus stopped on the corner where a crowd of people got on.

---

**darse la mano**

(idiom)

**la fortaleza**

(noun)

**to be on strike**

Los obreros *están de huelga* porque quieren sueldos más altos.

The workers are on strike because they want higher salaries.

**fortress, castle**

La *fortaleza* El Morro es un punto de interés turístico en San Juan.

The El Morro fortress is a point of interest for tourists in San Juan.

---

**estar de huelga**

(idiom)

**el embotellamiento**

(noun)

**to miss someone, something**

Cuando me mude, voy a *echarles de menos* a las comidas caseras de mi madre.

When I move, I am going to miss my mother's homemade meals.

**traffic jam**

Es casi imposible ir al centro por la tarde debido al *embotellamiento* en la carretera.

It is almost impossible to go downtown in the afternoon because of the traffic jam on the highway.

**echar de menos**

(idiom)

**el presupuesto**

(noun)

**whose**

Debemos mucho al sol *cuyos* rayos de energía nos dan vida.

We owe a lot to the sun whose rays give us energy.

**budget**

Los universitarios tienen que seguir un *presupuesto* limitado ya que la matrícula es alta.

Universities must stick to a limited budget since the tuition is already high.

---

**cuyo**

(*adj.*)

**el gerente**

(noun)

**twisted; sprained**

Alejandro andaba con muletas porque tenía el tobillo *torcido.*

Alejandro walked on crutches because he had a sprained ankle.

**manager**

Exijo que el *gerente* se encargue de mi reclamo urgente.

I demand that the manager take charge of the urgent complaint.

---

**torcido**

(*adj.*)

## la sospecha

(noun)

---

**false, fake, artificial**

Se notaba que la concursante llevaba pestañas *postizas*.

One could detect that the contestant was wearing false eyelashes.

**suspicion**

Aunque el abogado dijo que su cliente era inocente, había mucha *sospecha* por parte del público.

Although the lawyer said that his client was innocent, there was a lot of suspicion on the part of the public.

**postizo**

(*adj.*)

**el hueso**

(noun)

**deep**

El volcán creó una laguna muy *honda*.

The volcano created a very deep lagoon.

**bone**

A Rosario se le fracturó un *hueso* de la muñeca patinando sobre hielo.

Rosario broke a bone in her wrist ice skating.

---

**hondo**

(*adj.*)

**el sueldo**

(noun)

**grated; shredded**

El cocinero agregó queso *rallado* a la lasaña.

The chef added grated cheese to the lasagna.

**salary**

El jefe le dio un aumento de *sueldo* porque Pilar había vendido una gran cantidad de anuncios para el periódico.

The boss gave her an increase in salary because Pilar had sold many advertisements for the newspaper.

**rallado**

(*adj.*)

**la gripe**

(noun)

**pleasant**

Gozamos de unas vacaciones muy *placenteras* en San Juan.

We enjoyed a very pleasant vacation in San Juan.

**flu**

Ha habido una falta de vacunas para la *gripe* por lo que cuesta producirlas.

There has been a shortage of vaccines for the flu because of the cost to produce them.

**placentero**

(*adj.*)

## **el cuadro**

(noun)

---

**vigilant, awake**

La familia se quedó *desvelada* toda la noche cuando se murió su bisabuelo.

The family stayed awake all night when their great-grandfather died.

**painting**

Los *cuadros* negros de Goya son unos de los más conocidos del mundo.

Goya's black paintings are some of the most famous in the world.

---

**desvelado**

(*adj.*)

**la costumbre**

(noun)

**dyed**

Casi no reconocí a Margarita porque tenía el pelo *teñido*.

I almost didn't recognize Margarita because her hair was dyed.

**custom**

La quinceañera es una *costumbre* que conservan muchas familias hoy en día.

The "Sweet 15 Party" is a custom that is preserved in many families today.

**teñido**

(adj.)

**el cariño**

(noun)

**boiled**

La ensalada mixta lleva huevo *hervido*.

The tossed salad has boiled egg in it.

**affection, love**

Les tengo mucho *cariño* a mis nietos cuyas sonrisas son encantadoras.

I feel great affection for my grandchildren whose smiles are enchanting.

---

**hervido**

(adj.)

**la ley**

(noun)

**smoked**

El salmón *ahumado* está muy sabroso.

The smoked salmon is very tasty.

**law**

Aunque la *ley* es severa, hay que obedecerla.

Although the law is severe, it is necessary to obey it.

**ahumado**

(adj.)

**la fiebre**

(noun)

**conniving; tricky**

Me di cuenta de que el mago era algo *embustero* porque el truco no salió bien.

I noticed that the magician was somewhat conniving because the trick didn't turn out well.

**fever**

Héctor padecía de una *fiebre* alta y de escalofríos.

Hector suffered from a high fever and chills.

---

**embustero**

(adj.)

**la cuerda**

(noun)

**harmful**

Se ha comprobado que el usar tabaco es *nocivo* para la salud.

It has been proven that using tobacco is harmful to your health.

**rope**

Montaron la tienda de campaña con estacas y *cuerdas* fuertes.

They set up the tent with stakes and strong ropes.

**nocivo**

(adj.)

## el obrero

(noun)

**shed [blood, tears]; spilled**

Las lágrimas *derramadas* son amargas, pero más amargas son las que no se derraman. (Proverbio irlandés)

Tears shed are bitter, but even more bitter are those not shed. (Irish proverb)

**worker**

Hubo una huelga de *obreros* y se pararon todos los servicios de transporte.

There was a workers' strike and all the transportation services stopped.

---

**derramado**

(adj.)

## el secuestro

(noun)

**erased**

Casi no se ve la imagen en la fotocopia porque está casi *borrada*.

You can barely see the image in the photocopy because it's almost erased.

**kidnapping, hijacking**

Para prevenir un posible *secuestro* del avión, tuvimos que pasar el equipaje a mano por los rayos X.

To prevent a possible airplane hijacking, we had to pass the carry-on bags through the X-ray machine.

---

**borrado**

(adj.)

## el vidrio

(noun)

**wrong, mistaken**

Perdóneme, señora operadora, tengo el número *equivocado.*

Excuse me, operator, I have the wrong number.

**glass**

Muchos peces tropicales se podían ver a través del *vidrio* del acuario.

Many tropical fish could be seen through the aquarium's glass.

---

**equivocado**

(adj.)

**la antigüedad**

(noun)

---

**disgusting, sickening**

No me gusta la comida de esa cafetería porque la comida es *asquerosa*.

I dislike the food in that cafeteria because the food is disgusting.

**antique**

En el mercado de pulgas, me compré una *antigüedad* del siglo XIX.

At the flea market, I bought an antique from the 19th century.

---

**asqueroso**

(adj.)

**el desfile**

(noun)

**defeated, conquered**

Una vez *vencidos*, los soldados se dirigieron a la casa.

Once defeated, the soldiers headed home.

**parade**

Durante la celebración, se puede ver el *desfile* de carrozas desde este balcón.

During the celebration, you can see the parade of floats from this balcony.

**vencido**

(adj.)

**la multa**

(noun)

**necessary**

Es *preciso* que solicites un visado para viajar al Brasil.

It is necessary to apply for a visa to travel to Brazil.

**fine, ticket**

El policía le puso una *multa* por exceso de velocidad.

The police gave him a ticket for speeding.

**preciso**

(adj.)

# la montaña rusa

(noun)

**fixed; firm; secure**

No regatees en la tienda ya que los precios están *fijos.*

Don't haggle over the prices in the store since they are fixed.

**rollercoaster**

De todas las atracciones en el parque, a Ana le fascinó más la *montaña rusa*.

Of all the attractions in the park, Ana was most fascinated with the rollercoaster.

**fijo**

(adj.)

**la peluca**

(noun)

**bland**

Pásame la sal, por favor. Estos macarrones están muy *sosos*.

Pass the salt, please. This pasta is very bland.

**wig**

Casi no se le notaba la *peluca* porque era el color natural de su pelo.

It was almost impossible to tell it was a wig because it was the natural color of her hair.

---

**soso**

(adj.)

**el crepúsculo**

(noun)

---

**annoying; silly**

Ese tipo es *necio* porque siempre se porta muy mal.

That guy is annoying because he's always misbehaving.

**dusk, twilight**

Estaba muy oscuro en la calle hasta que los faroles se encendieron al *crepúsculo*.

It was very dark in the street until the streetlights came on at dusk.

---

**necio**

(adj.)

**el derecho**

(noun)

**dry**

El desierto Atacama en Chile es el más *seco* del mundo.

The Atacama Desert in Chile is the driest desert in the world.

**right [to do something]**

La primera enmienda de la constitución nos da el *derecho* de libertad de palabra.

The First Amendment of the Constitution gives us the right to free speech.

---

**seco**

(adj.)

**ahorrar**

(verb)

**heavy; dull**

Aun el hombre más fornido no pudo levantar el sofá *pesado*.

Even the most muscular man couldn't lift the heavy sofa.

**to save [money or time]**

Ya que se van subiendo los gastos, es preciso *ahorrar* dinero para el futuro.

Since the expenses are increasing, it's necessary to save money for the future.

**pesado**

(adj.)

**sobrevivir**

(verb)

**left-handed**

El pícher de los Cachorros es *zurdo*.

The pitcher for the Cubs is left-handed.

**to survive**

Los naufragados *sobrevivieron* en la isla por meses comiendo sólo frutas y nueces.

The shipwrecked men survived on the island for months, eating only fruit and nuts.

---

**zurdo**

(adj.)

**hacer daño**

(verb)

**noisy**

Los niños siempre son muy *ruidosos* cuando salen a jugar.

Children are always noisy when they go out to play.

**to damage, to harm**

El huracán le *hizo* mucho *daño* al centro de la ciudad; muchos edificios se destruyeron.

The hurricane caused a lot of damage in the center of the city; many buildings were destroyed.

---

**ruidoso**

(adj.)

**envolver**

(verb)

---

**naïve**

Para su edad, Paula es una persona bastante *ingenua*.

For her age, Paula is a rather naïve person.

**to wrap up**

Ya le compré un regalo de cumpleaños a Cecilia; sólo hace falta *envolver*lo.

I already bought a present for Cecilia's birthday; now I only need to wrap it.

---

**ingenuo**

(adj.)

**alejarse de**

(verb)

**smart, brilliant; of genius**

Alvarito es *genial;* siempre ha sido un niño precoz.

Alvarito is brilliant; he has always been a precocious child.

**to draw away from; to distance oneself**

No *te alejes* tanto *de* la orilla del mar, hijo; el agua está muy brava.

Don't go so far from the shore, son; the water is very rough.

---

**genial**

(adj.)

**atreverse a**

(verb)

---

**ferocious, savage**

El domador le dio un bistec al león *feroz.*

The lion tamer gave the ferocious lion a steak.

**to dare to**

Alejandro no *se atrevió a* llamarle a Martina porque era muy tímido.

Alejandro didn't dare to call Martina because he was very shy.

**feroz**

(adj.)

**regañar**

(verb)

**right-handed**

Todos en mi familia son *diestros* salvo mi hermanita, quien es zurda.

Everyone in my family is right-handed except my little sister, who is left-handed.

**to scold**

*Regañé* al perrito por haber hecho un lío en la sala.

I scolded the little dog for having made a mess in the living room.

**diestro**

(adj.)

**trasladarse**

(verb)

**weak**

Porque Rogelio había estado enfermo por varios días, todavía estaba *débil* cuando regresó al trabajo.

Because Rogelio had been sick for several days, he was still weak when we returned to work.

**to move**

La familia Torres *se trasladó* a la capital hace dos años.

The Torres family moved to the capital two years ago.

**débil**

(adj.)

**fallar**

(verb)

**day-to-day, routine, quotidian**

Todos en nuestra casa están acostumbrados a una rutina *cotidiana*.

Everyone in our house is accustomed to a daily routine.

**to fail [at an attempt]; misfire; malfunction**

Este reloj siempre me *falla*; es la tercera vez que se ha parado.

This clock always fails me; it is the third time that is has stopped.

**cotidiano**

(adj.)

**rendirse**

(verb)

**expensive**

Mi abuelo me regaló un reloj *caro* para mi Bar Mitzvah.

My grandfather gave me an expensive watch for my Bar Mitzvah.

**to surrender**

A los dos días del bombardeo, las tropas *se rindieron* al enemigo.

After two days of siege, the troops surrendered to the enemy.

**caro**

(adj.)

**lograr**

(verb)

**tied up; bound together**

Dejamos el bote de remos *atado* al tronco de un árbol en la orilla.

We left the row boat tied to the trunk of a tree on the shore.

**to achieve, get, obtain**

Los policías *lograron* capturar al fugitivo cuando entraron por la puerta trasera.

The police were able to capture the fugitive when they entered through the back door.

**atado**

(adj.)

**asegurarse de**

(verb)

**burning; passionate; fervent**

En la película *Como Agua Para Chocolate*, Tita sintió un amor *ardiente* por Pedro.

In the movie, *Like Water for Chocolate*, Tita felt a burning passion for Pedro.

**to assure; to make sure**

El contador *me aseguró (de)* que mis ahorros ganaran más intereses en otra cuenta bancaria.

The accountant assured me that my savings would earn more interest in another bank account.

**ardiente**

(adj.)

**deceased**

Los mexicanos suelen colocar ramos de flores en las tumbas de sus antepasados *difuntos*.

Mexicans tend to place flowers on the graves of their deceased ancestors.

**soler**

(verb)

**to tend to, to be in the habit of**

*Suele* haber un aguacero casi diariamente en la primavera.

There tends to be a rain shower almost every day in the spring.

(adj.)

**difunto**

**escoger**

(verb)

**someone else's**

Es maleducado meterse en los asuntos *ajenos*.

It is bad-mannered to get involved in someone else's affairs.

**to choose**

Es difícil *escoger* entre tantos postres tan ricos.

It is difficult to choose between so many tasty desserts.

**ajeno**

(adj.)

## evitar

(verb)

---

**sharp**

El pescador usó un cuchillo *agudo* para preparar los pescados que había cogido.

The fisherman used a sharp knife to prepare the fish that he had caught.

**to avoid**

Para mantenerse en buena forma, *evite* las comidas que contienen mucha grasa.

To stay in shape, avoid meals that contain a lot of fat.

**agudo**

(adj.)

**devolver**

(verb)

**quiet; taciturn**

No es que Angélica sea antipática sino que es una niña *taciturna* e introvertida.

Angélica isn't so much unpleasant as she is quiet and introverted.

**to return [an object]**

Puesto que no había *devuelto* mis libros a la biblioteca a tiempo, me cobraron sesenta centavos.

Since I had not returned my books to the library, they charged me 60 cents.

**taciturno**

(adj.)

**apagar**

(verb)

**short-lived; ephemeral**

Dicen que uno debe aprovecharse de la juventud ya que es muy *efímera.*

People say that one should enjoy one's youth since it is very short-lived.

**to turn off**

Les pedí a los vecinos que *apagaran* la música porque ya era muy tarde.

I asked the neighbors to turn off the music because it was very late.

**efímero**

(adj.)

**hallar**

(verb)

---

**banal; unoriginal; ordinary**

La última novela que empecé a leer tenía una trama tan *banal* que ni siquiera la acabé.

The last novel that I started to read had a plot so unoriginal that I didn't even finish it.

**to find**

Gustavo recibió una recompensa por haber *hallado* la sortija perdida.

Gustavo received a reward for having found the lost ring.

**banal**

(adj.)

## encargarse de

(verb)

---

**didactic, intended to instruct**

Las fábulas *didácticas* que leía de niño se me han grabado en la memoria.

The didactic fables that I read as a child have stayed in my memory.

**to take charge of**

Amelia *se encargó de* todos los detalles para la quinceañera de su hija.

Amelia took charge of all the details for her daughter's Sweet 15 Party.

**didáctico**

(adj.)

**criar**

(verb)

**capricious, whimsical**

Los pícaros de Murillo son algo *caprichosos* con sus cara risueñas.

Murillo's rogues are somewhat whimsical with their smiling faces.

**to raise [a child, animal]**

*Criar* a un hijo sano exige mucho por parte de los padres.

To raise a healthy child demands a lot on the part of the parents.

**caprichoso**

(adj.)

**espantar**

(verb)

**controversial, polemic**

Los senadores siguieron discutiendo un asunto *polémico* hasta la madrugada.

The senators continued discussing a controversial issue until dawn.

**to frighten**

Tenemos un gato muy tímido; se *espanta* al ver un ratoncito.

We have a very shy cat; it frightens him to see a mouse.

---

**polémico**

(adj.)

**realizar**

(verb)

---

**anxious**

Siempre me pongo *ansioso* si tengo que hablar en público.

I always get anxious when I have to speak in public.

**to accomplish; to carry out; to fulfill**

Ganar el Premio Nobel es algo que muy pocos pueden *realizar*.

Winning the Nobel Prize is something very few people can accomplish.

**ansioso**

(adj.)

**plantear**

(verb)

**moved [emotionally]**

El público estaba tan *conmovido* por el acto final de la ópera que todos salieron del teatro sin decir nada.

The public was so moved by the final act of the opera that they all left the theater in silence.

**to plan; to state, to pose an issue**

El conferenciante nos *planteó* dos asuntos polémicos para debatir.

The lecturer posed to us two controversial points to debate.

**conmovido**

(adj.)

## hospedarse

(verb)

---

**unfathomable, inscrutable**

La teoría que el profesor explicaba me pareció *insondable* puesto que yo no sabía mucho del tema.

The theory that the professor explained seemed unfathomable since I didn't know much about the subject.

**to house; to be lodged**

Nos *hospedamos* en una cabaña rústica cuando fuimos a cazar.

We were housed in a rustic cabin when we went hunting.

**insondable**

(adj.)

**aguantar**

(verb)

---

**idle; leisurely**

El tiempo *ocioso* resultó menos tranquilo de lo que nos imaginábamos.

The leisure time turned out to be less peaceful than we had imagined.

**to tolerate; to endure**

Baje el volumen. No puedo *aguantar* más ese ruido.

Turn down the volume. I can't tolerate that noise any longer.

---

**ocioso**

(adj.)

**engañar**

(verb)

**unfortunate; unlucky; unhappy**

Arturo estaba *desdichado* al enterarse de que no se había ganado la lotería.

Arturo felt unhappy when he learned that he hadn't won the lottery.

**to deceive, to trick**

No te *engañes* con todo lo que lees en las noticias.

Don't deceive yourself with everything that you read in the news.

**desdichado**

(adj.)

**entregar**

(verb)

**altruistic**

Los miembros de la iglesia eran muy *altruistas* en ayudar a los sin casa.

The church members were very altruistic in helping the homeless.

**to deliver; to hand in; to hand over**

Espero que me *entreguen* los muebles antes de que nos mudemos al nuevo apartamento.

I hope that they deliver the furniture before we move to the new apartment.

**altruista**

(adj.)

## abarcar

(verb)

**spoiled (child)**

Los hijos de María Elena son tan *mimados* y malcriados; ella los deja hacer cualquier cosa sin decirles nada.

María Elena's sons are so spoiled and badly behaved; she lets them do anything they want without saying anything.

**to encompass; to embrace**

La exhibición de pintura española *abarca* desde el Siglo de Oro hasta la época contemporánea.

The Spanish painting exhibition encompasses the Golden Age up to the current period.

**mimado**

(adj.)

## soltar

(verb)

---

**defeated; exhausted**

Después de ganar el triatlón, Raúl estaba *rendido* y casi no pudo caminar.

After winning the triathlon, Raúl was exhausted and almost couldn't walk.

**to turn loose; to let go of**

No quise *soltar* la mano de mi hijita en la muchedumbre cerca del accidente.

I didn't want to let go of my little daughter's hand in the crowd near the accident.

**rendido**

(adj.)

**burlarse de**

(verb)

---

**greedy**

El millonario *avaro* nunca se contentó por más dinero que tuviera.

The greedy millionaire was never satisfied no matter how much money he had.

**to make fun of**

En su novela, la autora *se burló del* materialismo en la sociedad de hoy día.

In her novel, the author made fun of the materialism in today's society.

**avaro**

(adj.)

**scared; frightened**

El gato *asustado* se escondió debajo del sofá cuando oyó la ambulancia.

The frightened cat hid under the sofa when it heard the ambulance.

---

**arrojar**

(verb)

**to throw**

El socorrista le *arrojó* un chaleco salvavidas cuando se cayó del muelle.

The lifeguard threw him a life vest when he fell off the pier.

**asustado**

(adj.)

**suceder**

(verb)

**daring, mischievous**

El niño *travieso* se llevó dos galletas sin que su niñera lo viera.

The mischievous boy took two cookies without his babysitter seeing him.

**to happen**

Jamás sabremos lo que *sucedió* porque no hubo testigo alguno del crimen.

We'll never know what happened because there was no witness to the crime.

---

**travieso**

(adj.)

## matricularse

(verb)

**light [in weight]**

Ya que la caminata era tan larga, decidí llevar una mochila *ligera*.

Because it was going to be a long walk, I decided to take a light knapsack.

**to enroll**

Aunque me han aceptado a varias universidades excelentes, no sé en cuál *me matricularé*.

Although several excellent universities accepted me, I don't know which one I will enroll in.

**ligero**

(adj.)

## asistir a

(verb)

---

**fastidious; excessively meticulous**

Ella era tan *fastidiosa* que pasaba la aspiradora dos veces al día.

She was so fastidious that she vacuumed two times a day.

**to attend**

*Asistí a* todas las reuniones del comité para estar enterado de sus planes.

I attended all the committee meetings in order to be informed of their plans.

**fastidioso**

(adj.)

**dirigirse**

(verb)

**wise, sagacious**

Tomé muy en serio el consejo del anciano ya que se le consideraba muy *sagaz.*

I took the advice from the elderly person very seriously since he was considered to be very wise.

**to address; to head out for**

Los pioneros *se dirigieron* al oeste en busca de oro en el siglo XIX.

The pioneers headed West in search of gold in the 19th century.

**sagaz**

(adj.)

**soñar con**

(verb)

**brazen; audacious**

El reportero nos ofendió con sus comentarios *descarados* sobre los desamparados.

The reporter offended us with his brazen comments about the homeless.

**to dream of**

Aunque no tiene suficiente dinero ahora, Ernesto *sueña con* comprar esa sortija para su novia.

Although he does not have enough money now, Ernesto dreams of buying that ring for his girlfriend.

**descarado**

(adj.)

**fallecer**

(verb)

---

**blind**

Dicen que fijarse en el sol durante mucho tiempo puede causar que uno se ponga *ciego*.

It is said that staring at the sun for a long time can cause you to go blind.

**to pass away**

Mi bisabuelo *falleció* hace mucho tiempo debido a un infarto.

My great-grandfather passed away long ago due to a heart attack.

**ciego**

(adj.)

**prestar**

(verb)

**swollen**

Se le torció el tobillo jugando al fútbol y luego se le quedó *hinchado*.

He twisted his ankle playing soccer and later, it became swollen.

**to lend**

Como el carro de Julio estaba en el taller, le *presté* el mío.

Since Julio's car was in the shop, I lent him mine.

**hinchado**

(adj.)

## renunciar

(verb)

**capital [letter]**

En el formulario hay que escribir su apellido en letras *mayúsculas*.

On the form it is necessary to write your last name in capital letters.

**to resign [from a job]**

Cuando se le ofreció el puesto como gerente, Anabel *renunció* de su trabajo como secretaria.

When she was offered the job as a manager, Anabel resigned from her job as a secretary.

---

**mayúscula**

(adj.)

**agarrar**

(verb)

---

**disguised; dressed as**

No reconocí a Lupe cuando salió al escenario porque estaba *disfrazada* de bruja.

I didn't recognize Lupe when she came on stage because she was dressed as a witch.

**to grab; to catch**

El águila *agarró* el ratoncito con sus talones y se lo llevó.

The eagle caught the mouse in his claws and took him away.

**disfrazado**

(adj.)

**rehusar**

(verb)

---

**native of**

Como era *oriundo* de Puerto Rico, no necesitaba pasaporte para entrar en los EEUU.

Since he was a native of Puerto Rico, he did not need a passport to enter the United States.

**to refuse**

Emilio *rehusó* aceptar el puesto como contador porque el sueldo era muy poco.

Emilio refused to accept the job as an accountant because the salary was quite low.

**oriundo**

(adj.)

**apetecer**

(verb)

**proud**

El padre se sentía muy *orgulloso* de su hija mientras ella cantaba con el coro.

The father felt very proud of his daughter while she sang with the choir.

**to crave; to hunger for**

Después de hacer ejercicios siempre me *apetece* un refresco frío.

After exercising, I always crave a cold drink.

---

**orgulloso**

(adj.)

**reduced; discounted**

Decidí comprar dos lámparas porque estaban bastante *rebajadas*.

I decided to buy two lamps because they were substantially discounted.

---

**toser**

(verb)

**to cough**

Jaime estuvo resfriado y pasó toda la noche *tosiendo*.

Jaime had a cold and he spent all night coughing.

**rabajado**

(adj.)

**repartir**

(verb)

**delayed**

Porque estuvimos *demorados* en el aeropuerto, perdí mi vuelo a Canadá.

Because we were delayed in the airport, I missed my flight to Canada.

**to distribute**

Le di una propina al muchacho que *reparte* los periódicos porque es muy responsable.

I gave a tip to the boy who distributes the newspapers because he is very responsible.

---

**demorado**

(adj.)

**arrancar**

(verb)

---

**careless**

A mi parecer, has limpiado la sala de una manera *descuidada* porque todavía hay polvo en los muebles.

In my opinion, you have cleaned the living room in a careless manner because there is still dust on the furniture.

**to start [a car]; to tear out; to rip out**

Tuve que *arrancar* las malas hierbas del jardín porque se veían tan feas.

I had to rip out the weeds in the garden because they looked so ugly.

**descuidado**

(adj.)

**coquetear**

(verb)

**tied [score]**

Después de una hora, los dos equipos permanencieron *empatados* uno a uno.

After an hour, the two teams remained tied one to one.

**to flirt**

La vio *coquetear* cuando le guiñó desde el otro lado del salón.

He saw her flirting when he winked at her from the other side of the room.

**empatado**

(adj.)

**sobornar**

(verb)

**sultry**

Debido a la humedad el clima es *bochornoso* en el Caribe.

Due to the humidity the climate is sultry in the Caribbean.

**to bribe**

No puedo creer que los fanáticos *hayan sobornado* al guardia para que los dejara entrar al concierto.

I cannot believe that the fans bribed the guard to let them into the concert.

---

**bochornoso**

(adj.)

## regatear

(verb)

**widowed**

Rafael estuvo *viudo* por diez años antes de volver a casarse.

Rafael was widowed for 10 years before remarrying.

**to haggle; to bargain**

Como no había precios fijos en el mercado, teníamos que *regatear* con los vendedores.

As there weren't fixed prices in the market, we had to bargain with the vendors.

---

**viudo**

(adj.)

**jactarse de**

(verb)

---

**available**

Cuando llegamos al teatro a las ocho el acomodador nos indicó las butacas *disponibles*.

When we arrived at the theater at eight o'clock, the usher showed us the available seats.

**to boast, to brag**

En la reunión, todos los jefes se *jactaban de* sus sueldos altos y autos caros.

In the meeting, all the bosses bragged about their high salaries and expensive cars.

(adj.)

**disponible**

## adivinar

(verb)

**seasick; dizzy**

Casi todos los pasajeros del buque se pusieron *mareados* porque había olas tan altas.

Almost all the passengers of the boat became seasick because there were such high waves.

**to guess**

Si de veras sabe el truco, *adivine* qué naipe tengo aquí en la mano.

If you really know the trick, guess which card I have in my hand.

---

**mareado**

(adj.)

**fingir**

(verb)

**educated, refined, cultivated**

Me parece que ella es muy *culta* porque sabe tanto de la ópera.

It seems to me that she is very cultivated because she knows so much about opera.

**to fake, to conceal, to pretend**

Alberto *fingió* tener sueño durante la conferencia, pero de hecho lo oyó todo.

Alberto pretended that he was sleepy during the lecture, but in fact he heard everything.

**culto**

(adj.)

**lastimar**

(verb)

**cautious**

El ladrón era muy astuto y *cauteloso* porque no dejó huella alguna.

The burglar was very keen and cautious because he did not leave any fingerprints.

**to hurt**

La mejilla sangrienta denotó que el soldado se había *lastimado*.

The bloody cheek indicated that the soldier had been hurt.

---

**cauteloso**

(adj.)

**prender**

(verb)

**welcoming, warm, cozy**

Esa familia es muy *acogedora* ya que siempre nos brinda su hospitalidad.

That family is very welcoming since they always offer their hospitality.

**to turn on; to ignite**

Antes de la barbacoa, *prendimos* la parrilla.

Before the cookout, we lit the grill.

**acogedor**

(adj.)

## vacilar

(verb)

**demanding**

El doctor Mújica es un profesor muy *exigente*; hace que sus alumnos escriban una tesis para sacar una nota sobresaliente.

Doctor Mújica is a very demanding professor; his students have to write a thesis to get a high grade.

**to hesitate; to vacillate**

Los jueces *vacilaron* durante una hora antes de tomar una decisión.

The judges hesitated for an hour before making a decision.

**exigente**

(adj.)

**actualizar**

(verb)

**retired**

Una vez *jubilado*, Jorge se dedicó a jugar al golf.

Once retired, Jorge dedicated himself to the game of golf.

**to update**

Debo *actualizar* mis archivos en este ordenador porque hace tiempo que no los abro.

I should update my files on this computer because I have not opened them in a while.

**jubilado**

(adj.)

**ensayar**

(verb)

**indispensible; necessary**

Es *imprescindible* llevar botas en la selva tropical porque hay mucho lodo en el sendero.

It is necessary to take boots to the tropical rainforest because there is a lot of mud in the path.

**to rehearse**

Los actores *ensayaron* con los cantantes para el espectáculo.

The actors rehearsed with the singers for the show.

**imprescindible**

(adj.)

**llenar**

(verb)

**sequestered; hijacked; kidnapped**

El jurado se mantuvo *secuestrado* para que no vieran las noticias durante el juicio.

The jury was kept sequestered so that they wouldn't see the news during the trial.

**to fill up**

Hazme el favor de *llenar* el tanque con gasolina sin plomo, por favor.

Do me a favor and fill up the tank with unleaded gas, please.

---

**secuestrado**

(adj.)

## alcanzar

(verb)

**svelte; gracefully slender**

El jaguar *esbelto* corre por la selva tropical persiguiendo su presa.

The gracefully slender jaguar runs through the tropical rainforest pursuing its prey.

**to reach; to attain, to catch up with**

Corrí para *alcanzar* al joven que dejó caer su billetera.

I ran so that I could catch up with the young man who dropped his wallet.

---

**esbelto**

(adj.)

**encender**

(verb)

**bald**

Mi abuelito es casi *calvo*; usa una peluca todos los días.

My grandfather is almost bald; he wears a wig every day.

**to turn on; to light**

*Encendieron* las velas del pastel de cumpleaños de Eulalia.

They lit the candles on the cake for Eulalia's birthday

---

**calvo**

(adj.)

**acertar a**

(verb)

**daring, bold**

Aun enfrentado con un feroz león, el domador pareció ser muy *atrevido*.

Despite being face to face with a ferocious lion, the trainer seemed very bold.

**to guess correctly; to hit the mark**

*Acertó a* dar en el centro del blanco dos veces seguidas.

He happened to hit the center of the target two times in a row.

**atrevido**

(adj.)

## acordarse de

(verb)

**defeated**

En la ronda final, las campeonas fueron *derrotadas* por dos goles.

In the final round, the champions were defeated by two goals.

**to remember**

No me *acordé de* la letra de la canción cuando llegó el momento de cantarla.

I didn't remember the words of the song when it came time to sing it.

---

**derrotado**

(adj.)

**carecer de**

(verb)

---

**hidden**

El mapa indica donde está *escondido* el tesoro.

The map indicates where the treasure is hidden.

**to lack**

*Carecen de* lo más sencillo para vivir acomodados.

They lack the most basic things to live comfortably.

---

**escondido**

(adj.)

## depender de

(verb)

**exhausted, used up**

Después de trabajar doce horas seguidas, la enfermera estaba *agotada*.

After working 12 hours straight, the nurse was exhausted.

**to depend on**

La boda será al aire libre o en la capilla; todo *depende del* tiempo.

The wedding will be outdoors or in the chapel; it all depends on the weather.

**agotado**

(adj.)

## despedirse de

(verb)

**burned**

Después de pasar todo el día en la playa, los bañistas estaban *quemados* por el sol.

After spending all day at the beach, the sunbathers were burned from the sun.

**to say goodbye**

Los padres *se despidieron* de su hijo en el campamento de verano.

The parents said goodbye to their son at summer camp.

---

**quemado**

(adj.)

**entretener**

(verb)

**distinguished, outstanding**

Antonio Gaudí fue un arquitecto muy *destacado* del siglo XX.

Antonio Gaudí was a very distinguished architect from the 20th century.

**to entertain**

Los muchachos se *entretuvieron* jugando por horas en la computadora.

The boys entertained themselves playing for hours on the computer.

---

**destacado**

(adj.)

**extrañar**

(verb)

**stubborn**

Mi hermanito es tan *testarudo*; no escucha a nadie.

My little brother is so stubborn; he doesn't listen to anybody.

**to miss; to long for**

Voy a *extrañar* a mi hija cuando se vaya para la universidad.

I am going to miss my daughter when she goes to college.

**testarudo**

(adj.)

**gozar de**

(verb)

**tight**

Me duelen los pies; estos zapatos están muy *apretados*.

My feet hurt; these shoes are very tight.

**to enjoy**

Aunque mi abuelita tiene noventa años, ella *goza de* buena salud.

Although my grandmother is 90 years old, she enjoys good health.

**apretado**

(adj.)

**wide**

Con sus doce carriles, la Avenida 9 de julio es la más *ancha* del mundo.

With 12 lanes, the 9 of July Avenue is the widest in the world.

**asombrarse**

(verb)

**to frighten; to astonish**

Los ladrones se *asombraron* y huyeron cuando se abrió la puerta.

The thieves were astonished and fled when the door opened.

---

**ancho**

(adj.)

**fomentar**

(verb)

**involved**

El alcalde estaba *involucrado* en la política municipal antes de ser elegido.

The mayor was involved in municipal politics before being elected.

**to foster; to encourage**

Una dieta equilibrada y el ejercicio *fomentan* la buena salud.

A balanced diet and exercise foster good health.

---

**involucrado**

(adj.)

**perezoso**

(adj.)

---

**thick**

Una merienda típica en España consiste en churros con chocolate caliente y *espeso*.

A typical snack in Spain consists of churros with hot and thick chocolate.

**lazy**

Alfredo nunca tiene ganas de trabajar; es más *perezoso* que un vagabundo.

Alfred never has a desire to work; he is lazier than a vagabond.

**espeso**

(adj.)

**célebre**

(adj.)

**cheap, inexpensive**

El chicle es tan *barato*. Se vende a 25 centavos la docena.

The gum is so cheap. It's 25 cents a dozen.

**famous**

El *célebre* palacio de la Alhambra se encuentra al pie de la Sierra Nevada.

The famous palace, the Alhambra, is found at the foot of the Sierra Nevada.

---

**barato**

(adj.)

## soltero

(adj.)

---

**friendly, amiable**

Mi vecina es tan *amable*; siempre me trae postres caseros.

My neighbor is so friendly; she always brings me homemade desserts.

**single, not married**

Como es *soltero*, tiene menos responsabilidades que sus amigos casados.

Since he is single, he has fewer responsibilities than his married friends.

**amable**

(adj.)

**grabado**

(adj.)

**distant**

Los novios piensan casarse en el futuro *lejano*.

The couple plans to marry in the distant future.

**recorded, taped**

La versión *grabada* de la canción era distinta a la versión cantada en vivo.

The recorded version of the song was different than the version heard live.

**lejano**

(adj.)

## **vencido**

(adj.)

**renowned, well-known**

Gabriel García Márquez es un escritor colombiano muy *reconocido* universalmente.

Gabriel García Márquez is a universally renowned Colombian writer.

**defeated, conquered; worn out**

La victoria fue fácil una vez que se vio su espíritu *vencido*.

The victory was easy once their spirit was defeated.

**reconocido**

(adj.)

# convencido

(adj.)

**stupid; foolish**

Nadie es tan *insensato* como para querer lesionarse, así que se recomienda que se abroche el cinturón de seguridad.

Nobody is so foolish as to want to get hurt, therefore it's recommended that you fasten your seatbelt.

**convinced**

A pesar de la evidencia en su contra, Miguel estaba *convencido* de que tenía razón.

In spite of the evidence to the contrary, Miguel was convinced that he was right.

---

**insensato**

(adj.)

# ubicado

(adj.)

**vast, ample, spacious**

El garaje es tan *amplio* como para que quepan dos vehículos grandes.

The garage is large enough to fit two full-size cars.

**situated; located**

El hotel está *ubicado* en el centro; está cerca de los puntos de interés turístico.

The hotel is located in the city center; it is near the touristic points of interest.

---

**amplio**

(adj.)

**manchado**

(adj.)

**wet**

Luisito se resbaló en el piso *mojado*.

Luisito slipped on the wet floor.

**stained, soiled**

Se le cayó mostaza en el suéter y se le quedó *manchado* aun después de llevarlo a la tintorería.

She dropped mustard on her sweater; it remained stained even after taking it to the dry cleaner.

**mojado**

(adj.)

**adinerado**

(adj.)

---

**unbearable**

El calor de Andalucía en verano es *insoportable*.

The heat in Andalusia in the summer is unbearable.

**wealthy, well-to-do**

Las mansiones que vimos en la Avenida Central nos aseguraban que estábamos en un residencial muy *adinerado*.

The mansions that we saw on the Avenida Central assured us that we were in a wealthy residential neighborhood.

---

**insoportable**

(adj.)

# ABOUT THE AUTHOR

**Ken Stewart** teaches AP Spanish Language at Chapel Hill High School in Chapel Hill, North Carolina. He is a National Board Certified Teacher in World Languages. He is a graduate of UNC–Chapel Hill with degrees in International Studies and Spanish, having studied in Seville and Salamanca, Spain. Mr. Stewart has served as content editor to AP Central™ and has been an AP reader, table leader, and College Board consultant for 13 years. He is the author of an AP Spanish manual for Duke University and The Golden Age Art of Spain. He has been named Spanish Teacher of the Year for North Carolina and the Central North Carolina Teacher of the Year.

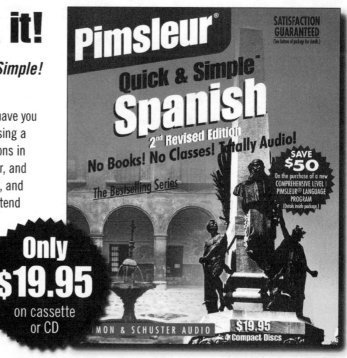